Becky - Ma
Comfort you ?
ahead.   Love
Pat

A Different Season

A Practical Guide for Growth While Grieving a Death

Joseph Robert Pfeiffer, LCSW, GT.

Josh R. Pfeiffer

Publisher's Cataloging-in-Publication
(Provided by Quality Books, Inc.)

Pfeiffer, Joseph R.
    A different season: a practical guide for growth while grieving a death / Joseph Robert Pfeiffer. – 1st ed. (2nd printing 2000)
    p. cm.
    Includes index.
    Preaasigned LCCN: 96-80107
    ISBN 0-9655865-2-9

    1. Bereavement–Psychological aspects. 2. Bereavement–Religious aspects–Meditations. I. Title

BF575.G7P44 1997   155.937
                            QBI97-40466

Book design by: Virginia Donelson Curry

ATTENTION SCHOOLS, ORGANIZATIONS, AGENCIES, AND CHURCHES: Quantity discounts are available on bulk purchases of this book for gift giving, fundraising or educational training purposes. For information contact:
Marketing Department, Landscapes Publishing,
P. O. Box 820650 Memphis, Tennessee 38182-0650
(901) 578-9107; E-mail: Sales@LandscapesPublishing.com

Contents

Preface

Introduction and Benefits From This Book

Author's Note

About The Author

Dedication

Acknowledgments

Section 1 – Chilling Visions of Wintertime

Section II – Evolving Landscapes of Autumn

Section III – Reaping the Harvest of Summer

Section IV – Surprising Moments of Springtime

Index

Preface

In over 20 years of counseling hundreds of grieving people, it has been my experience that during a major loss individuals remain in a state of shock for a prolonged period of time. This numbing effect inhibits one's ability to absorb a lot of information. One task for me as a counselor is to teach. During loss, I strongly believe that "less is more." Too much information is unproductive, and it is more effective to give individuals a small amount of practical advice to aid their grief recovery.

My experience with grieving people also has taught me another valuable lesson: spirituality for many people is central to surviving mentally and emotionally difficult times. This book offers meditations based from the Psalms as a constant reminder of God's love for us, and of God remaining very present to us during loss. The meditations in this book can also be a starting point for individuals to add to or to write their own.

The death of significant others in our lives affects us profoundly. I believe that people have come into my life for many reasons: to teach, to comfort, to support, to challenge.

The death of my parents, Rose and George; my friends, Jim and Helene; my nephew, Mark; and my aunt, Betty, have helped me to grow in ways I never imagined.

This book is not only a tribute to them but also a testament to all those people who have allowed me to walk with them through their pain.

Introduction

This book is about hope and healing. To grieve is to truly grow. If you have lost someone from death, you live the pain; if you know someone experiencing the loss of a loved one, you know of their pain.

Often people who seek counseling ask me to help them take away their pain and to do it quickly. Crazy as it may seem to those experiencing it, without such depth of pain growth will be minimal. Pain incites, motivates and stretches us in ways unknown. Loss creates discomfort, and it is this discomfort that people often seek to eliminate as soon as possible.

The most important step you can take during grief is to know what to expect and then become actively involved in your recovery. Your grief is a personal and individual journey which will be full of emotions, however, there will come a time when hope prevails.

This book, *A Different Season*, is not like the four seasons in nature that you have experienced, for it does not follow the logical sequence as you know it. I have *intentionally* rearranged the seasons because that is the way people feel and act during the beginning of their grief. Life's course is very much changed. In addition to presenting brief, practical steps to use while grieving, this unique book includes meditations.

In the *Chilling Visions of Wintertime,* the starkness of gray skies adds to the fact that death throws us into shock and confusion; there is numbness and intense pain. Life is "on hold," and this season best describes how one's life feels disconnected.

The course of grief changes as one moves into the ***Evolving Landscapes of Autumn***, surrounded by bold, fiery orange and red leaves, you find yourself immersed with many changes. Life is full of uncertainty and doubt, and you remain unsettled and feel very uprooted.

As you move into the next season, you find yourself evolving, sometimes painfully and slowly. In ***Reaping the Harvests of Summer***, the green landscape emanates hope, but bittersweet times remain full of laughter and sadness. You continue to seek peace while feeling very different from your way of living before this death occurred.

Walking into the last season, ***Surprising Moments of Springtime,*** there is a profusion of color like a rainbow; you discover your life undergoing many transformations and new beginnings. Life fills with renewed hope as you continue to change and grow and mourn your loss.

Although your grief is unique, most of us pass through four passages during the seasons of our grief recovery: Validation, Readjustment, Reevaluation and Rebuilding. These passages are not necessarily sequential; but each step is critical in the recovery process.

🍂 *Validation* – a time to accept all of your feelings and allow them to be expressed in healthy ways.

🍂 *Readjustment* – a time to remain flexible while caring for yourself as you adjust to some fast-paced changes.

🍂 *Reevaluation* – a time for you to look at your life, attitudes and values, to once again determine what's important to you.

🍂 *Rebuilding* – a time which requires you to invest yourself in a new, different and meaningful lifestyle.

As you move through these passages, at your own pace, hopefully you will become more tolerant of yourself and understand what is happening to you.

At a service for my nephew, Mark, who was only eighteen years "too" old when he died, I was asked to lead those gathered in prayer. Realizing there were many denominations in the room, I wanted to somehow begin with a familiar song known by all. Old, tattered hymn cards were found, and the first song on the card was "Amazing Grace." I said to those gathered that all our lives are full of grace and love. For those who knew Mark, he was truly amazing grace. I asked everyone to sing, but I wanted to make a change in a verse–the one stanza on the card read, "that saved a wretch like me," and I said to those gathered, "let's change that and sing 'that saves and sets me free,' because we are not a wretched people, and certainly God wants all of us to be free."

After the service a woman came to me, sobbing profusely. I didn't know her, but she said, "I want you to know that what you said to us this evening lifted a burden of twenty-five years off my shoulders, and I am deeply grateful." I didn't know this woman's burden, but I did know at that moment that this amazing thing called grace did indeed happen. My hope is that you also will be filled with "amazing grace"–to be healed and set free.

–*Joseph R. Pfeiffer*

Benefits You Will Receive from this Book

- Brief, specific information that is easy to understand.
- Clearer comprehension of your grief recovery.
- Practical strategies to help you deal with your pain.
- Meditations to comfort your spirit.
- A self-assessment inventory to chart your progress.

Author's Note

This book is intended for adults experiencing the recent death of a significant other: spouse, parent, sibling, grandparent, friend, partner, or child.

To those of you who grieve, I can only attempt to fully understand what is happening in your life; loss is a universal experience which connects us all as humans. Approach this book like a road map, for you are on a personal journey of grief. There are many ways to travel. The terrain may be unfamiliar and even perilous. At what pace you travel and reach your destination is up to you.

🍃 *There are important things you can do that will be helpful in your journey. There are things that are self-destructive.*

🍃 *You are encouraged to actually __say__ the words aloud where indicated.*

🍃 *Carry this book with you as long as your grief remains with you. There will come a time when you will put this book away.*

🍃 *Leave this book on your desk while at work. Read and reflect daily. Those who see the book may use the occasion to talk to you about your loss.*

🍃 *You can read one entry daily or weekly. You may want to peruse the book in one sitting to get a better understanding of what you will encounter.*

🍃 *Use this book in whatever way works best for you. Remember there is more than one way to use this book.*

🍃 *Complete the self-assessment inventory at the end of each section to monitor your growth.*

Joseph Robert Pfeiffer, L.C.S.W., GT, is a licensed clinical therapist, nature photographer, writer, multi-media producer and grief therapist with over twenty years of grief counseling experience. Joe has conducted educational programs on loss and uses a variety of creative expressions in his grief work. Joe is a speaker and consultant in the fields of clinical social work and human development. His deep passion for the earth has resulted in simple photographed moments of nature for others to delight in and enjoy and also inspired him to develop the theme of his book, *A Different Season: A Practical Guide for Growth While Grieving a Death.* He is also the author of a creative, practical resource titled, *Bereavement Handouts* (reproducible educational handouts for clients).

Dedication

Dedicated To My Nephew
Mark William Pfeiffer
July 6, 1968–September 22, 1986
Who died at the tender age of 18 in a tragic accident.
A young man full of caring, warmth and humor.
and
To all parents who have lost
a Most Special Gift
Their Child.

Acknowledgments

I owe much to those people who assisted me throughout this endeavor. Special thanks to Tom Bird, author and teacher, who propelled me into my dream of writing this book.

A host of people were critical editors: Joel Chapman, Susan Erdman, Sister Delores Montini, David O'Grady, Jane Hampshire and Larry Lambert. I thank them for their valuable insight and comments.

To all those who helped with layout, design, editing and proofreading: Norm Shaw, Gloria White and Virginia Curry. Thanks also to Mark Faris for his artistic illustrations.

To those numerous individuals and families I have counseled over the years. I have always believed that I am not only a teacher to them but a student who learns a great deal from the sharing of their personal experiences of grief and loss.

Finally, to my best friend, Kent Usry, who has been at my side giving me his constant hope, encouragement, and love.

Professional Help

Important: This book is not a substitute for professional counseling or medical care. This book is sold with the understanding that the publisher and the author are not engaged in rendering professional services.

If psychological or any other type of expert help is required, the services of a competent professional should be sought.

Healing Prayer For Those in Grief

God, do not let my feelings
overwhelm me.
During moments of anguish
touch my heart with courage,
my soul with your compassion
and with your love comfort me.
Despite my pain let me know
healing is occurring.
Let me hear often that you
are always with me.
God, today is different, I am
faced with many changes.
Help me to know
I am not powerless
and that I am surviving.
Give me hope for tomorrow.
Let me believe in myself and
allow others to comfort me.

                                    Amen.

 **𝓑ereavement 𝓔xpress**

A heartfelt way to express your condolences
to a relative, friend, co-worker or client.
Send a copy of this book, along with a message
from you personally handwritten on a card.
A Different Season is autographed by the
author and gift wrapped.
Sent USPS Priority Mail to the bereaved.

**When words don't seem enough
your gift of *A Different Season*
will help say what is in your heart.**

See order form in back of book.

Section I

Chilling Visions of Wintertime

Give Yourself Permission to Grieve ———— page 17

The Feeling of Falling Apart ———————— page 19

Pain, Pain Go Away———————————— page 21

Intruding and Unwanted Thoughts————— page 23

How Long Will This Grief Last?——————— page 25

Embracing All of Your Feelings —————— page 27

Feeling Wounded and Different —————— page 29

Being Human ————————————— page 31

Self-Talk ———————————————— page 33

Addictions to Live Without ———————— page 35

Depression —————————————— page 37

Getting the Help You Need ———————— page 39

Self-Assessment Inventory———————— page 40

Chilling Visions of Wintertime

*T*here is a finality during this season
　 of nature; it is an ending:
shocking, frigid temperatures,
faded remains of flowers that once bloomed,
trees completing their seasonal cycle.

*B*leakness confronts me.
　 Dreary days seem to last forever.
Gray, skies encircle me.
Ice and cold sum up this season of the year.
There is a starkness not experienced during any
other season.
Nature is extremely tested,

and so am I.

*L*ike winter there is a stillness in my heart.
　 Time seems suspended.
I am flooded with emotions, I am overwhelmed.
Life as I have known it has been shattered.
So many thoughts and feelings seize me.
I know this thing called loss.
I am shocked and devastated.
Like barren trees, I feel lifeless;
and most of all,

I feel abandoned.

Prayer

God, I ask you,
Why has this happened?
I don't understand.
I am overwhelmed with feelings.
Words can't express what I feel.
I am numbed and shocked.
I need to know that you hear me.

Give Yourself Permission to Grieve

Say: Whatever I am feeling now is okay, even if
I believe my feelings are terrible.

What you are experiencing is called "GRIEF," and it
is pain-filled. Grief, although it doesn't seem like it now,
is a temporary condition. You may be experiencing a
variety of symptoms: anguish, deep sorrow, remorse,
sadness, shock, disbelief, anger, numbness, loss of
appetite, lack of energy, and a tiredness that sleeping
doesn't help.

You are experiencing an emotional wound. You may
feel overwhelmed. You are not crazy. This is normal.
A death creates great discomfort resulting in much
change. Your life as you once knew it appears very
different. It is quite normal for you at this time not to
know or understand.

The Good News:

Your grief will pass one day.

Prayer

God, I keep saying, "I can't believe this has happened!" There must be some mistake.
Is this a joke or a dream?
I am at a loss for words. I don't know what to do.
I want to cry and I can't. I'm confused.
What did I do to deserve this?
I have many questions, and there are no answers.
God, do you hear me? In my deepest sorrow
and pain, where are you, God?

The Feeling of Falling Apart

Say: All loss creates a condition of grief; this is
a normal occurrence.

Feelings of irrationality and absurdity bombard
you. You are overwhelmed. Decision-making is difficult,
communicating with others strenuous. Disorganization
and confusion best describe your life. Completing
routine tasks seems nearly impossible. You feel clumsy.

Grieving has a way of tearing you down emotionally and physically. All of this is temporary. Even though
this is a new experience, you will work through this pain.

The Good News:

**By living one day at a time, you discover
simple ways to cope with devastating times.**

Prayer

God, who can measure the depth of my
pain and anguish?
Who but you knows of my true
feelings and misery?
I ask for the wisdom and strength
to move through this time of grief.

Pain, Pain, Go Away

Say: I have the ability and inner resources to deal with my pain and survive this loss.

You may want to avoid your pain rather than face it (by overindulging in too much work or activities). If you choose this path you can be assured that your pain will literally eat away at you, affecting you emotionally, physically, spiritually and in other ways you least expect.

You also may fear that your pain may never leave. Seldom does this occur. Illogical and unreasonable fears don't materialize as imagined.

During this time of loss, you are experiencing many intense feelings. Your pain may sear you like a raw wound. Remember, wounds heal. Healing seldom happens at the pace you would like it to happen. With self-care, nurturance, understanding and the time you need to grieve, healing occurs.

The Good News:

By walking with your pain, you will one day walk out of it.

Prayer

God, sometimes I feel that
you are asleep.
In the face of
fear-filled moments,
all of my life as I know it
seems threatened.
Why am I
bombarded by so many thoughts?
In the midst of self-doubt,
help me, God, to discover
that in turning to you
I will be comforted.

Intruding and Unwanted Thoughts

Say: Things seldom happen the way I imagine.

Loss affects your normal way of thinking. More than likely you are finding it difficult to concentrate and may find yourself thinking, "I won't be able to live through this loss, I can't take it." You may be constantly questioning yourself. All of this can affect your self-esteem, add to guilt and give rise to negative thinking (constant thoughts of being worthless now that your loved one has died). This negative thinking is normal during grief, however, you can let it paralyze you or turn your thoughts into motivation.

Explore the use of self-talk. Every time you find yourself being negative, too harsh on yourself or obsessively thinking about the "what if's," stop mid-thought or shortly afterward. Say to yourself out loud something positive, like: "I am doing okay, and I will make it through this." You want to counteract your negative put-downs with positive affirmations.

The Good News:

By allowing yourself the opportunity to grieve, everyday will be a day of healing.

Prayer

God, I feel so broken and wounded.
I am devastated by this loss.
Let me discover your stronghold,
a grace and presence that will
be with me during
my time of grief.

How Long Will This Grief Last?

Say: I grieve now; placing it on hold will only create problems for me.

You may wonder, "Will this pain and hurt ever end? When will these intense feelings cease?" Placing a time frame on your recovery may set you up for disappointment, if you're not finished with your mourning once that time has arrived. Grief recovery takes time–anywhere from months to years. Although the intensity of your feelings will decrease over time, remember, your sadness will be transformed into a deeper understanding of your loss.

The Good News:

Your grief recovery is very different than anything you have experienced.

Prayer

God, I feel like I am being
pulled in many directions.
So many of my feelings
just come and go.
Strangely, I feel alone,
and yet you are always with me.

Embracing All of Your Feelings

Say: If I repress my feelings I will give them power; if I embrace them I gain strength.

You have experienced a major loss in your life. Although individuals respond to loss in many ways, there are similar characteristics felt by everyone. Some of what you are feeling may seem strange or frightening. Don't run from any of your feelings; this is not healthy. Even though you may not be able to name the feelings you are experiencing, they belong to you, and all of them are okay.

Understand that there are healthy and destructive ways to deal with your feelings. It's important to learn the difference. Befriend your feelings; they have something to teach you. Do not repress or be frightened by any of your emotions; trust your own feelings and intuition. It is important that you acknowledge all of what you are feeling and experiencing.

The Good News:

The intensity of what you are feeling will eventually diminish.

Prayer

During this time of trouble,
God, remind me often
that in the midst
of my vulnerability,
you also
give me hope and grace
to face today and tomorrow.

Feeling Wounded and Different

Say: My vulnerability will decrease as time passes.

Re-living each moment of the death in your mind can be very painful, and yet, it actually helps you to begin to deal with your loss. All of the feelings you are experiencing are common to those who grieve. There is no need to be ashamed of any of your feelings. Repressing your feelings can hurt you emotionally. Don't allow others to tell you how you should grieve.

It is not unusual when you first learn about the loss of your loved one to experience a very surrealistic moment. You feel there are "two parts" of yourself – one is reality: you continue to do things; and the other is detached: you watch things unfolding. Remember, this is a way for you to deal with the enormous pain of your loss.

The Good News:

By allowing yourself to feel different you are healing yourself.

Prayer

I feel like I am living my life
in a vacuum, God.
My life is changed,
and it is difficult for me
to accept this loss.
During my grieving help me realize
I am always in your loving care.

Being Human

Say: Grief is a vital part of being human.

Your life as you once lived it seems to have been blown apart like a bomb. During your time of grieving, however, the world doesn't stop. Life moves along at its own fast pace. Things may not seem real to you at times.

Each death is very different, yet shares a similar grief response. Grieving is individual and personal. Dealing with the reality of your loss requires patience. Don't try to rush this process or discount what you are feeling. Discover your own style of grieving and coping, and use it to your advantage.

The Good News:

Your human nature gives you all the inner resources you need to survive this loss.

Prayer

God, I cry out to you
with all of my fears and worries.
Help me remind myself
often that you are with
me, easing my anxieties.

Self-Talk

Say: One goal of grieving is to resolve my loss and to reconstruct my new life.

When someone leaves you, it is easy to think, "How will I survive?" or "How will I make it through all of this?" Your way of thinking can easily become illogical and circular, increasing your fears and raising your anxieties.

Your thoughts don't need to control you; they can be mastered because they are only thoughts, yet what you tell yourself does affect the way you feel and ultimately how you act. Positive thoughts do bring about positive change.

The Good News:

As you gradually change, your grief changes too.

Prayer

My body aches, God,
and I want something to help ease my pain.
I pray for peace and rest.
God, touch my soul and remind me
that you are a place
of caring refuge.

Addictions to Live Without

Say: Taking a detour around my feelings will only lead me on a deceptive journey.

During initial stages of loss expect your body to be assaulted by many emotional and physical symptoms.* Your sleeping and eating patterns are affected you may feel lethargic, restless, and irritable.

You wonder if you will be able to bear this pain and you may turn to temporary solutions. Overindulging in alcohol, drugs or food, may temporarily make you feel better but you only put off the inevitable, and even more damaging you delay your recovery process.

The Good News:

The symptoms of grief you now experience will decrease in time.

*Refer to page 125,
Appendix A: Possible Symptoms of Distress Related to Loss

Prayer

God, the source of all love,
during this time of loss,
I cry out to you.
In my distress, comfort me.
During my loneliness, be my companion.
During my distress,
be my source of faith.

Depression

Say: Now is not the time for me to be heroic.

Perhaps the most difficult aspect of loss is how to deal with depression. Feelings of helplessness and hopelessness, despair, sadness and having a heavy heart linger. You feel drained.

Depression often accompanies a major loss.* Depression is a chemical reaction in your body to a situation or event, which also has an emotional and spiritual component. Willing your depression to go away doesn't work.

Do your basic needs prevent you from functioning well? Does prolonged deprivations of sleep, nutrition or meaningful work interfere with your basic functioning? A visit to your primary care physician or a psychiatrist to evaluate your symptoms and medical needs may be appropriate. Medication, counseling and supportive therapies can be very helpful.

The Good News:

There is help available for your dramatic mood swings, which will change over time.

*Refer to page 126,
Appendix B: Signs to Look for When Depressed

Prayer

God, I feel like
I'm wandering and lost.
Let me see the light of my faith.
Let me allow others
to care for and comfort me,
knowing that they come
in your name.
For you have not left me
to face this loss alone.

Getting the Help You Need

Say: Others can help or be a hindrance to my grief recovery. I will surround myself with helpers.

You may at times choose to do nothing with the way you feel or think. However, keep in mind that you do not have to endure all of what you're feeling and going through alone.

Because you are very vulnerable at this time, your impulse may be to distance yourself from others to prevent yourself from being hurt any further. But it's important to work through your hurt and pain rather than keep it inside. Seeking out a trusted friend, clergy person, professional counselor or support group can help you heal.

The Good News:

You remain the best "expert" of what you need by listening to your body and caring for it.

🍃 Self-Assessment Inventory 🍃

Feelings

How Am I Feeling?   10 9 8 7 6 5 4 3 2 1

Easy to Identify   Don't Know
                                                    What I Am Feeling

Thinking

What I Am Thinking?   10 9 8 7 6 5 4 3 2 1

Extremely   Extremely
Positive   Negative

Coping

How I Am Coping?   10 9 8 7 6 5 4 3 2 1

Appropriately   Inappropriately
Healthy   Destructive

Self-Talk

What Am I Saying To Myself? 10 9 8 7 6 5 4 3 2 1

Very   Extremely
Affirming   Defeating

Support

How Much Support
Do I Have In My Life?   10 9 8 7 6 5 4 3 2 1

Tremendous   No Support
Amount of Support

Anger

What Intensity of Anger
Do I Have?   10 9 8 7 6 5 4 3 2 1

None   Furious

Section II

Evolving Landscapes of Autumn

Transformations _____ page 45

If Only _____ page 47

Making Yourself Well _____ page 49

To Be Comforted _____ page 51

Looking at Your Expectations _____ page 53

Fears _____ page 55

The Anger Within _____ page 57

Returning to Normal _____ page 59

Life "On Hold" _____ page 61

Secondary Losses _____ page 63

Family and Friends Grieve, Too _____ page 65

What's Helpful to You? _____ page 67

Self-Assessment Inventory _____ page 68

Evolving Landscapes of Autumn

*A*utumn is a season in process.
Nature is unfinished.

*F*aced with a tableau of changing colors,
scurried by a bewilderment of movements, what
we see today is gone tomorrow.
We know what is going to eventually occur, but never
quite sure of when or how.

*T*he barrel of fresh apples is not quite full, the work
not yet completed.
Leaves hang on wind-strewn branches not wanting to let go.
Neither do I.

*L*ike autumn, I am surrounded by the inconsistencies
of sadness and joy, despair and hope, hate and love.

*T*his leave-taking and separation is marked with pain
of autumn's ultimate end.
Like leaves blowing in the wind,
I feel uprooted and unsettled.
I am tired and fatigued.
Dreary and wind-chilled days "drag me down."
I'm obsessed about my loss.
Fears control my thoughts.
Wanting to let go to find peace,

I don't feel whole.

Prayer

God, during this time
of so many changes,
help me cope.
I find it difficult
to embrace
all these changes.

Transformations

Say: I am undergoing numerous changes; I will not make any major decisions at this time.

How you deal with your grief response depends upon several things: the circumstances of your loss, your relationship to the one you lost, your personality, your state of health, how you have previously faced loss, your religious beliefs and spirituality, and how you choose to respond to your loss.

Remember, your grief response affects you emotionally, spiritually, physically and sexually. During the throes of grief, you can make choices about how you will respond.

The Good News:

By taking some small steps each day, you will work through your grief.

Prayer

My God, as I seek understanding
let me be comforted.
Help me to blame less.
By trusting in you
may I discover
meaning.

If Only

Say: While I am grieving, thinking about all the *"If only's"* is nonproductive.

Blaming is usually an attempt to restore a sense of control over life. Blaming yourself and others gives you a false sense of control.

You may find yourself bombarded with "If only's." "If only I could have been with him," or, "If only I had done more for her." If this occurs, do the following: counteract the blaming with a statement of what you have done or actions that you have performed. Substituting these words or something similar will counteract illogical and unreasonable thinking and will help restore some balance. Remember, the passage of time will eventually restore your sense of control.

The Good News:

There is a meaning to your loss.

Prayer

God, grant me
peaceful rest.
Revitalize me.

Making Yourself Well

Say: Doing too much can make me ill.

Loss zaps your emotional and physical health. This remains a vulnerable time for you. Trying to do too much can make you susceptible to illness. Now is the time to be extremely kind to yourself.

The Good News:

Resting enables you to maintain a positive attitude, which greatly influences your health and aids in the healing process.

Prayer

God, help me to know
often that you are
my constant source of hope.
Comfort me with your love.
Reassure me with your grace.

To Be Comforted

Say: The one I lost will always remain with me.

Everywhere you go your grief follows you. You are reminded of your loss and feel the pain often. Your heart is restless for that familiar voice and face. The silence of the moment can be deafening knowing your loved one is gone forever, yet, it is comforting to know how much you loved each other. Remembering is bittersweet, consoling and painful. No one can ever take those memories away from you.

The Good News:

The grieving you are faced with today will one day change.

Prayer

My God, I have little idea
where my life is headed.
I can't see far in front of me,
and there's much uncertainty.
During these stormy days,
be my refuge and anchor.

Looking at Your Expectations

Say: I am able to take charge of my life
if I choose to.

You can never fully prepare yourself for a loss. What you can do now is seriously look at the expectations you place on yourself.

Be realistic and accept your humanity. Live today without trying to solve all your problems.

Grief work is full of pain and can seem frighteningly endless. It isn't. Don't place too many expectations on yourself, for it will make you anxious. You are surviving and healing.

The Good News:

You are in control of the choices you make.

Prayer

God, do not allow my fears
To control me.
So many of my fears are
imagined or irrational.
Help me to know every
moment of the day,
that you are with me
and I need not be afraid.

Fears

Say: Loss can make me believe I am out of control and helpless.

The fear of the unknown can cripple you and become paralyzing. You are not powerless over your fears. The trauma of this loss may lead you to believe that you will never get over today and never be able to face tomorrow.

Fears cloud your awareness, especially because you are experiencing so many intense feelings. Fears can be real or imagined. Most fears imagined never happen. By believing in yourself, you empower yourself. By acknowledging your fears, you feel less powerless over your loss. When you identify and name your fears, they become less frightening.

The Good News:

You are stronger than you believe, and you possess the inner resources to face your fears and heal.

Prayer

God, I am sometimes so afraid
of my anger. I'm afraid that if
I really become angry,
I'll lose control and unleash
a monster within me.
Help me accept that anger
is just another emotion,
and that I need to express it
in a healthy way to benefit me.

The Anger Within

Say: To be angry is human; to discount anger hinders my grief recovery.

Anger is essential to acknowledge and deal with. These emotions may be new to you and even frighten you. Anger can be used to cover up your pain and vulnerability. Anger can block your efforts to appropriately deal with your grief in a healthy way.

If you refuse to talk about your anger and ignore your feelings you deny an important part of your humanity. Anger can be expressed in many healthy ways. Use them to your good.

The Good News:

Anger, when acknowledged and expressed is very cleansing and healing.

Prayer

God, I attempt
to regain some normalcy,
but at times not much makes sense to me.
I am struggling so much with this loss.
Give me peace
and comfort.
As I continue to hurt,
be near me with your love.

Returning to Normal

Say: I will remain flexible in dealing with my
grief recovery.

You will struggle at times in being preoccupied
with your loss. You will remain overburdened. You may
think you don't have the strength to carry on. You
wonder if life will ever be normal again.

Grief is seldom resolved by yourself. As you engage
in activities at home and at work, you begin to see how
many changes you've made. Days turn into weeks,
weeks turn into months, and you realize how strong
you are and how far you have come.

The Good News:

In time your life will again become stable.

Prayer

God, my life continues
without my loved one. My life is very different.
Let me know that it is okay
to have so many questions and doubts.

Life "On Hold"

Say: I will not underestimate the trauma of
my loss.

When loss occurs – especially when it is sudden and
unexpected – you may become obsessed about the loss,
mulling over questions in your mind. "Why did this
happen? Why must I suffer?" You also may ask, "How
should I feel? What should I do?" Questioning and
seeking answers is very human. It is okay if you feel
your life is a nightmare that will never end.

The Good News:

**You remain capable in adapting to changes
during this time of stress in your life.**

Prayer

This loss, God, brings some other
memories to mind that
I have not thought
about for sometime.
Some of these memories
add to my sorrow.
May my faith in you and
belief in myself
allow me to grow from these memories.

Secondary Losses

Say: I will hold on to the belief that tomorrow
will be better than today.

It is obvious that your primary loss is the one who
died. There remain, however, other important losses
that may not be as obvious.

Your role is defined by those with whom you have
a relationship, and when relationships end the nature of
that relationship is altered. You no longer are with your
companion or best friend. All of your personal and
shared dreams, plans and hopes for the future are now
very different. These secondary losses accompany the
death of a loved one, leaving behind gaps in your life.

During this time it is also natural to recall other
past losses that may intensify your grief.

The Good News:

What is a burden today will one day change.

Prayer

God, remind me that others
grieve with me over this loss.
During these moments of anguish,
touch all our hearts with your
compassion, and comfort us
with your love.

Family and Friends Grieve, Too

Say: When I become comfortable with all of my feelings, I help others with the healing process.

You may find it difficult to help others understand your feelings. Remember that others around you grieve, too, and you can't "do" their grieving. Others may not be able to support you emotionally because they may not know how to reach out to you.

Some family members and friends may keep distance from you because they feel helpless. Some may feel angry over the loss and direct that anger toward you because you are still living.

The Good News:

As others mourn with you, allow them to grieve in their own way.

Prayer

God, help me discover
what is most helpful for me
during my grieving. Give me the
strength to remain
true to myself.

What's Helpful to You?

Say: I will find my own sources of support and use them.

Now is a good time to ask, "What really comforts me?" Family and friends usually have good intentions to help you, since it is not healthy to grieve a loss completely alone.

Grief presents you with reactions commonly experienced by others. Care for your own needs first. Your body, mind and spirit are a team; allow them to work together and don't ignore any areas.

In your search to remain true to yourself, you may find a need to deepen your faith life since your spirituality can provide you with hope and comfort.

Counseling may be a healthy choice under certain circumstances. It's a sign of good health if you choose to get involved in counseling and/or a support group.

The Good News:

The most loving tribute you can give to the one you lost is to be true to yourself.

❧ *Self-Assessment Inventory* ❧

Feelings
How Am I Feeling?

10 9 8 7 6 5 4 3 2 1

Easy to Identify   Don't Know
What I Am Feeling

Thinking
What I Am Thinking?

10 9 8 7 6 5 4 3 2 1

Extremely   Extremely
Positive   Negative

Coping
How I Am Coping?

10 9 8 7 6 5 4 3 2 1

Appropriately   Inappropriately
Healthy   Destructive

Self-Talk
What Am I Saying To Myself?

10 9 8 7 6 5 4 3 2 1

Very   Extremely
Affirming   Defeating

Support
How Much Support
Do I Have In My Life?

10 9 8 7 6 5 4 3 2 1

Tremendous   No Support
Amount of Support

Anger
What Intensity of Anger
Do I Have?

10 9 8 7 6 5 4 3 2 1

None   Furious

Section III

Reaping the Harvest of Summer

Stormy Conversions —————————————— page 73

The Challenges of Grief —————————————— page 75

Turbulent Moments —————————————— page 77

You Are Surviving —————————————— page 79

Control —————————————— page 81

Unfinished Business —————————————— page 83

Your Sexuality is Affected —————————————— page 85

Possessions —————————————— page 87

Guilt —————————————— page 89

Spirituality —————————————— page 91

Time —————————————— page 93

Remembering the Good Times —————————————— page 95

Self-Assessment Inventory —————————————— page 96

Reaping the Harvests of Summer

*N*umerous trees shade us from the
fiery sun of summertime.
Like a cocoon, tree leaves protect us from the rain.

*F*ields kneel before us, nourished by the sun,
as the work of our labor bears fruition.
We rejoice as choice crops are harvested.
A time of happiness and beauty,
the season of summer remains to be fulfilled,
and so do I.

*T*he signs of summer call me to celebrate.
Yet my heart remains restless. I am
cautious of the sun, which can easily harm me.

*I*n the storm-filled moments of nature,
tree branches are tossed — some broken.
The loss in my life still hurts.
I bend and will recover, for I remain rooted and strong.

*R*outine moments cause me to remember.
It is a bittersweet time.
My reminiscing surprises me with
laughter and happiness —
fleeting moments of better days
and a sadness which still remains.

I am searching and seeking
for something I do not know.

Prayer

God, help me keep alive
the knowledge that you are
always at my side,
with your loving care.
Remind me often that
you will never leave me.

Stormy Conversions

Say: There are healthy ways to embrace and adjust to my loss.

Loss is unavoidable. In nature, the continuation of life is dependent upon death. Paradoxically, new life only begins when death occurs. Allow this time for growth and discovery. Use this time to your advantage to learn about your emotions, spirituality, and relationship with self and others.

The Good News:

**The dark turbulent clouds of loss
will one day pass.**

Prayer

God, help me reach out for support
and strength. Give me hope as I learn
to laugh again and enjoy life.

The Challenges of Grief

Say: I will help myself by accepting all of who I am.

Grief is a paradox; the more you grieve the easier it becomes in carrying your burdens and healing your hurt. No one in life escapes the experience of loss. Accept your limitations, go slow as there are no "quick fixes" in resolving your loss and pain.

By wearing a symbol of mourning – e.g. a black ribbon on your clothing – you make others aware of your loss and your hurt on the inside. The symbol encourages others to talk to you. This exchange is an important part of your healing.

The Good News:

Grieving occurs with small steps and not with leaps and bounds.

Prayer

God, as I vacillate between
restlessness and serenity,
let me hear and know
that you are
always near me.

Turbulent Moments

Say: Without warning, I can expect to experience emotional flashbacks.

As you continue to move through your grief, change continues to occur. As you become more familiar with your loss, you will feel in control one day and on a emotional roller-coaster ride the next. These rapid changes may happen without much warning. All of what is happening to you is a reminder that your grief remains. It is also a reminder that your healing continues.

The Good News:

Intense feelings will surface, yet know they are short-lived.

Prayer

Give me moments of simplicity, love,
laughter and hope.
Help me, God, to open my eyes
and see the wonder in you
and others who surround my life.

You Are Surviving

Say: I have the strength to move through all the
seasons life gives to me.

Every day that passes is one day closer to full
healing. This doesn't mean that you won't feel sadness
or pain. It does mean that you will continue to gain
strength and confidence in yourself.

What happens to you today will never quite happen
to you in the same way again. Tomorrow will be different. Don't dwell on the past or fear the future. Look at
today and all the choices available to you. You are
surviving and will continue to adapt.

The Good News:

Truth provides you with possibilities.

Prayer

God, let me know that it is
futile for me to control life.
Help me realize
that the one thing I can
always count on
is your constant love for me.

Control

Say: Control helps to regulate my anxiety.

Control. You use it daily, and yes, you need it. Too much control hinders you, but too little control makes you feel anxious. The more change you face, the more you will find yourself attempting to control situations. Control helps you deal with your fears.

You may have thought you had life under control. Suddenly, you are faced with a loss and feel very vulnerable. Now you think you have little control. Actually, you do control how you think, feel and act. You have control over the choices you make daily.

The Good News:

Embrace all of who you are, and you will free yourself from too much control.

Prayer

God, this remains a difficult
time for me.
Life is unfinished.
I seek resolve and
need some peace.

Unfinished Business

Say: Life as I once knew it will never be the same.

You may experience difficulty in putting some closure to this relationship. There will be no more good-byes, expectations will never be fulfilled, and life will remain unfinished because the person who died is gone forever. You may continue to ask why this happened, yet, knowing the "why" would not necessarily make you feel any better and certainly doesn't change anything.

Saying good-bye in your own way and in your own time is important. It doesn't mean forgetting your loved one, but rather remembering the good and familiar times in your life.

The Good News:

Every time you can say good-bye, you validate the relationship you once had, and you continue to heal.

Prayer

God, you know me as I am.
I have many needs, and
I have yet to satisfy
all of what I desire.
May your love, for now, satisfy
my needs.

Your Sexuality Is Affected

Say: I will not deny any of my sexual feelings.

One goal of grief recovery is to integrate this loss in your life. The trauma of loss affects your sexuality. You may not want to admit it or think about this now. Whatever sexual relationship you once had is now gone. You may fear you'll never have a sexual relationship again.

You don't have to get all of your life worked out at this time. Because loss creates a great deal of stress, it's important to work on your inner grief. As you take on new relationships remember that your sexuality is an important part of who you are, and may take time to heal, too.

The Good News:

Your grief affects all of who you are, and that is to be expected.

Prayer

God, the possessions of my loved
one bring both joy and
sadness to my heart.
May they help me remember
and give thanks to you.

Possessions

Say: Reminders of my loss will be everywhere.

You may wonder what to do with personal effects and items. These possessions will be difficult to relinquish because they have a special connection to the one who died. These items seem to have a life-perpetuating power. You may wonder how you can give away such personal and meaningful items.

Consider setting up your own timetable for passing on some of these items. Do it at your own pace. Those items you want to keep and those you choose to give away are entirely up to you. Hold onto these possessions as long as you need.

The Good News:

The reminders that make you sad today will one day fill you with fond memories.

Prayer

God, as I deal with
my regrets,
help me accept that I am
imperfect and human.
Let me embrace all
of my unique gifts
and talents and use
them for my benefit
and yours.

Guilt

Say: I will play an active role in my grief recovery; I will not be a helpless bystander.

Sometimes guilt is very subtle and difficult to recognize. Listen to your self-talk. Is it full of blame?

If you seek to inflict pain on yourself for enjoying the simple things in life, if you constantly place unrealistic expectations on yourself, if you find yourself overly anxious or seek perfection at all costs, you are experiencing some degree of guilt.

If you truly have some regrets about what you may have said or done, or failed to do–admit it, accept it and let it go. Often the most difficult person to forgive is yourself. Hanging onto guilt is unhealthy and keeps your wounds open preventing you from growing and being who you really are.

The Good News:
By dealing with your guilt you encourage healing.

Prayer

God, there are many unanswered
questions in my life.
As I seek answers, help me to be patient.
Help me to know you are always
by my side, asking me to
place my trust in you. May
my faith be a steadfast presence of
hope and healing for me.

Spirituality

Say: I will take time to know the presence of God and the power of faith in my life.

God, or your faith, may seem very distant and unavailable or much closer to you during this time. Your life has changed; God's life hasn't.

God does not cause you pain. Loss, and the grief resulting from it, is a part of being human. The answers, comfort and peace you seek may not be forthcoming from God or others as quickly as you want.

Use this time to look at your relationship with God. Explore your faith and spirituality to once again acknowledge and affirm what's important to you. Faith and spirituality definitely possess healing powers. God's presence is always available without you ever asking for it.

The Good News:

**No matter how or when you pray,
you are being healed.**

Prayer

God, I wish this could
be a different time for me.
If I worry too much about the future
or regret too much of the past,
I simply fail to see this time in my life
as an opportunity
to better know myself and you.

Time

Say: Time does help heal, but in and of itself it doesn't make me feel better.

After all is said and done, there will come those moments that are full of routine, boredom and loneliness. You already are aware that your attitudes and thoughts influence your health and healing. The only certainty you have is what today gives you and how you respond.

These seemingly long moments or days will end. During this time continue to listen to what your body requires and respond to it. These moments are opportunities to rediscover yourself.

The Good News:

One thing you can be sure of, tomorrow begins a new day for you.

Prayer

God, as I remember
all the good times shared
with the one I lost,
let me celebrate that life with joy.
Thank you for the gift of memory.

Remembering The Good Times

Say: In the telling and retelling of my stories,
I heal.

After a while family and friends may not mention the name of your loved one for fear of upsetting you. Often others are uncomfortable with their own feelings.

Bittersweet moments will remind you of those gifts shared, and yet you will feel sadness. Expect this to occur for sometime.

When you do share your memories with those who listen and care, (about the death, what the person meant to you, how your life is going without your loved one physically present, how you are feeling) the gift lives on. Recall the many gifts that remain, and don't allow death to diminish any of them.

The Good News:

**Your loved one will always
remain part of your life.**

🍃 Self-Assessment Inventory 🍃

Feelings
How Am I Feeling?

10 9 8 7 6 5 4 3 2 1

Easy to Identify   Don't Know
What I Am Feeling

Thinking
What I Am Thinking?

10 9 8 7 6 5 4 3 2 1

Extremely   Extremely
Positive   Negative

Coping
How I Am Coping?

10 9 8 7 6 5 4 3 2 1

Appropriately   Inappropriately
Healthy   Destructive

Self-Talk
What Am I Saying To Myself?

10 9 8 7 6 5 4 3 2 1

Very   Extremely
Affirming   Defeating

Support
How Much Support
Do I Have In My Life?

10 9 8 7 6 5 4 3 2 1

Tremendous   No Support
Amount of Support

Anger
What Intensity of Anger
Do I Have?

10 9 8 7 6 5 4 3 2 1

None   Furious

Section IV

Surprising Moments of Springtime

Who Am I? —————————————————— page 101

Expect the Unexpected ————————————— page 103

Viewing Loss as a Teacher——————————— page 105

New Beginnings———————————————— page 107

Trusting————————————————————— page 109

Simple Truths ————————————————— page 111

Anniversaries ————————————————— page 113

Your Memory Book——————————————— page 115

The Paradox of Acceptance ————————— page 117

Growth Is More Than a Six Letter Word ——— page 119

The Meaning of Healing————————————— page 121

The Promise of Hope ————————————— page 123

Self-Assessment Inventory——————————— page 124

Appendix A —————————————————— page 125

Appendix B —————————————————— page 126

"The Song of My Mother"———————————— page 127

Index ————————————————————— page 128

Surprising Moments of Springtime

*U*nexpectedly, spring buds forth once again
with wonder and beauty.
The air fresh as the morning dew
gladdens the heart and soul,
the long, cold, winter now forgotten.

*B*arren trees one day, budding sprouts the next.
The landscapes filled with so much newness,
overshadowing those brief memories of
a sad and harsh winter.
Trees and plants, no longer the same as before,
have changed and grown,
And so have I.

I am overtaken with euphoric delight,
for barren dead-like branches bring forth
new life. Nature entertains me.
This is a sacred time

I pause to remember those yesterdays
of that cruel winter of loss that
now seems so long ago.
I have survived.
Like nature, it is a season of new beginnings.
Through my loss I better understand that
chilling wintertime of my life.
I still ponder about what will be,
but I am confident in this new season.

I feel hope.

Prayer

God, as I rediscover who I am
and what's important to me,
help me open my eyes
to life and all it has to offer.

Who Am I?

Say: I face a challenge everyday: living a new life without the person who was an important part of my life.

During this time you will continue to question many things. More than likely you will evaluate what is really important to you and look at what you need to change or release. Loss forces you to rethink how you view life and what is valuable to you.

As difficult as it may seem, your task is to see yourself without the other person in your life. This will require you to restructure your life, values, beliefs, and attitudes, as you once again discover who you are, what you need, and what is most important in your life, i.e. "Before my loved one died, I always thought I wasn't good at making friends, and now I find I am making new acquaintances and people seem to like my company."

The Good News:
During this stage of questioning and examination, you will discover what is important to you.

Prayer

God, as I remember,
let me know that you are
always with me
on my journey.

Expect the Unexpected

Say: I will not be surprised by sudden recurring reminders of my loss.

Though your life may seem more stable now, you may at times be overcome by strong emotions or recurring thoughts that remind you of your loss. It is normal to have these experiences. Acknowledge what is happening, and allow yourself to continue walking through your grief.

The Good News:

You know you have moved forward in your grief when you experience lapses of momentary pain and intense feelings.

Prayer

God, open my eyes and teach me
the wonders of creation. Help me
learn to accept the healing that
comes from you
through others.

Viewing Loss as a Teacher

Say: I will allow myself to explore life at this time.

You continue to grow as you uncover some basic truths during your healing process. Some of these truths include: what is gone was very important to you; loving always involves pain; you are a resourceful person; you can't control life but manage it; loss is never a punishment from God; you are wiser and richer.

The Good News:

**Being open to what life offers you
is deeply rewarding and exciting.**

Prayer

God, help me accept
the miracle of rebirth,
trusting that the future
is always in your hands.

New Beginnings

Say: I will keep an open mind to new ways of living and relating with others which I may have never attempted before.

As time moves forward you will be faced with new and varied choices. Change, no matter how positive, is difficult. How you view change is important. Is it a friend or foe?

Getting back into the "swing of things" is difficult, if not uncomfortable at best. Social gatherings, dinner parties and celebrations can be moments of loneliness or unexpected surprise. As you become involved in these events, remember your inner dialogue—your behaviors and actions correspond with your self-talk.

The Good News:

Every trauma resulting from loss carries seeds of devastation, as well as new meaning and hope.

Prayer

God, help me to trust you
as I experience new realities.
As I befriend myself and claim
my inner strength,
help me face the future with courage.

Trusting

Say: I believe in myself and will open my mind
   to possibilities.

Loss has a way of forcing you to face new realities.
There will be many times when you question or doubt
yourself. Strange as it may seem, questioning and
doubting is part of the grieving process. This process
requires courage and a recommitment to life itself.

When you befriend this ongoing movement instead
of viewing these new realities as a threat, you'll be
surprised at the inner strength you possess.

The Good News:

**All things are given to you for a reason.
Little happens by chance or fate.**

Prayer

Be with me on my journey,
God, as I continue to discover
simple truths.
Help me understand,
accept and be at peace with myself.

Simple Truths

Say: I learn from adversity; for it's a catalyst for rebirth.

As you begin to embrace loss as a friend, you will discover the opportunity to gain a deeper understanding and appreciation for life. Remember how far you have come: your grief reactions are much less intense, and the good days continue to surpass the bad. This remains a time of rebirth: life without your loved one is being experienced in a new way.

The fullness of spring has not yet arrived, thinking back you thought you would never make it this far. Painful moments of sadness remain as you continue to work on your inner grief. You discover you can endure and face the future.

The Good News:

By being vulnerable to pain your reward is to know love.

Prayer

God, assure me often,
especially during these times of
uncertainty and change.
Fill me with your
constant love.

Anniversaries

Say: I will allow others to respond to my needs during special days.

During the first and subsequent celebration of birthdays, holidays or special events after the loss of a loved one, expect your grief response to return briefly. This grief doesn't mean that the intense pain you first experienced during your loss is returning. During this time, be extra caring and understanding of yourself. Allow others to comfort you as well.

The Good News:

These moments are of short duration; be patient and they will pass.

Prayer

God, when I reflect on the past,
I remember the many
good times shared with the one I lost.
May I keep alive my memories
as I thank you for all
that was given to me.

Your Memory Book

Say: I honor the one I lost by letting him or her live in and through me.

Remembering is usually bittersweet–full of joy and sadness, delights and regrets. Mementos, items and belongings of your loved one provide solace and comfort. There remain creative ways to personalize your loss and pain.

Ask yourself: What gifts were given to me? What was unique about the person I lost? What will my loved one be remembered for? By keeping these meanings alive in some fashion, your loved one lives on. Art, a photo album, writing a biography, beginning a family history, planting a garden or tree, establishing a scholarship – these are a few of the many ways to create a tribute and remain connected to your loved one.

The Good News:
Love and memories remain forever.

Prayer

God, let me never grow weary with despair.
Help me to appreciate what life
gives me today and
to anticipate the future with hope.

The Paradox of Acceptance

Say: To love is never a mistake; failing to do so is.

There is little that will ever be able to replace the relationship you once had. It was "one of a kind." There will be a longing for your lost love. You may continue to seek a reason why this loss occurred.

In time, ironically, a purpose may find you. When you least expect it, discoveries will be revealed.

The Good News:

The farther you walk with the struggle of your loss, the easier it becomes.

Prayer

I give thanks to you, God,
for all the gifts in my life,
including the painful changes that
come my way.

Growth is More Than a Six Letter Word

Say: Pain teaches me many things and I will
also discover many inner resources I never
knew existed.

Growth occurs when you are open to the process–
even if it is painful. Getting back on your feet and
allowing the new you to emerge will happen when you
don't attempt to control or rush the process.

The Good News:

**Every day you continue to grow and change
for the better.**

Prayer

God, you direct my ways.
As I walk by the side of the road
lined with flowers and weeds,
help me see how much
I have grown and
am loved by you.

The Meaning of Healing

Say: I will hold onto my grief as long as I need to.

Don't be surprised if after months or years you unexpectedly become discouraged or depressed over the loss of your loved one. You think, "I should be over this" or, "something is wrong with me." You may fear what the future holds without your loved one, who was an integral part of your life.

To be healed does not mean you'll never feel any of your emotional wounds again. You will. Some of your brokenness is healed; other areas continue to require care.

The Good News:

Healing is a slow process, and many emotions can't be easily controlled during this time.

Prayer

God, continue to give me
new sights and sounds
full of surprise and wonder,
laughter and love.
Let me know that even unexpected
snowfall on spring flowers
is a surprise and a gift.

The Promise of Hope

Say: My moments of pain remain; however, they are different than before.

Hope is present when:

You appreciate life and all it offers you.

You experience a newness and insight about others.

Your awareness of others' pain and hurt is
more apparent.

You take risks in reaching out to others.

You are basically comfortable with who you are.

You have a greater appreciation for this moment in
time, knowing it could change tomorrow.

You know that life is worthwhile and full of promise.

You know that the future depends upon the choices
you make.

You are able to laugh at yourself and with others.

The Good News:

Spring brings the hope of new life as the harshness of winter is gone, for it is a different season.

🍂 Self-Assessment Inventory 🍂

Feelings
How Am I Feeling?

10 9 8 7 6 5 4 3 2 1

Easy to Identify   Don't Know
What I Am Feeling

Thinking
What I Am Thinking?

10 9 8 7 6 5 4 3 2 1

Extremely   Extremely
Positive   Negative

Coping
How I Am Coping?

10 9 8 7 6 5 4 3 2 1

Appropriately   Inappropriately
Healthy   Destructive

Self-Talk
What Am I Saying To Myself?

10 9 8 7 6 5 4 3 2 1

Very   Extremely
Affirming   Defeating

Support
How Much Support
Do I Have In My Life?

10 9 8 7 6 5 4 3 2 1

Tremendous   No Support
Amount of Support

Anger
What Intensity of Anger
Do I Have?

10 9 8 7 6 5 4 3 2 1

None   Furious

Appendix A

Possible Symptoms of Distress Related To Loss

Emotional
Excessive worry/anxiety
Preoccupation
Irritability
Easily angered
Moods change quickly
Withdrawal
Constant sense of fear or
    impending doom
Restlessness
General sadness
Discouragement

Mental
Lack of concentration
Boredom
Being too cynical
Being too negative
Confused/unfocused
Diminished productivity
Poor decision making
Forgetfulness
Little creativity

Spiritual
Loss of meaning
Questioning of faith
Anger at God
Apathy toward church
Unable to forgive
Emptiness
Becoming too religious

Physical
Change in eating patterns
Insomnia/sleeping too much
Accident prone
Stomach disturbances
Muscle aches
Ongoing fatigue
Change in sexual functioning

Note: If you already experience some of these symptoms prior to your loss, your symptoms may increase in frequency or intensity. In order to rule out any physical illness, it is suggested you speak with your primary physician about this.

Appendix B

Signs to Look For
When Depressed

- You have no desire to live.
- You feel like physically harming yourself or someone else.
- You find it extremely difficult to get out of bed.
- You find it very difficult to doing simple things.
- You find no pleasure in life.
- You have isolated yourself from others.
- You feel both helpless and hopeless.

Help is Available

**If you have been experiencing any
of these symptoms for more than
a few days, see a physician and/or a
professional counselor as soon as possible.**

The Song of My Mother

A Willow – born a tender Willow.
Composed of fragile leaves of love.
Ever bending and changing through the seasons
of her life – through the seasons of our lives.

Branching out to embrace all.
Weathering the storms of Spring–
             the heat of Summer–
             the cold winds of Autumn
             the harsh winter snows.

Growing, Growing,
and always deep-rooted in love.
Beautiful – Strong and Beautiful –

May we now become as Mighty Oaks but,
always, always holding a bough of the
gentle Willow close to our hearts – for you.

— *Barbara Ann Pfeiffer*

Read at the Resurrection Mass of her mother, Rose M. Pfeiffer
March 17, 1976.

Index

A

Acceptance-117
Activity, meaning of-5, 21, 59
Addictions-35
Anger. appropriate-57
Anniversary responses-113
Anxiety-33, 81, 89, 125
Assessment inventory-
    7, 8, 40, 68, 96, 124

B

Blaming-47, 89

C

Change-45, 77, 81, 101, 107, 125
Choices-45, 53, 79, 81, 107, 123
Choose-53
Confusion-19
Control-47, 55, 77, 81, 105
Counseling-12, 37, 67

D

Depression and signs-37, 126

E

Eating and grief-35
Emotional flashbacks-77
Emotional responses to grief-
    17, 27, 29, 35, 37, 57, 77,
    103, 121, 125
Energy, lack of-17
Expectations-53, 83, 89

F

Faith-67, 91, 125
Falling apart-19
Family grief-65, 95
Family support-65, 67, 95
Fatigue-125
Fears, related to loss-
    21, 55, 81
Feelings-
    17, 19, 21, 25, 27, 29,
    35, 37, 55, 57, 65, 77,
    95, 103
Forgiveness-89
Friends and support-
    39, 67, 95

G

Getting help-
    12, 37, 39, 67, 126
God
  Anger at-125
  Increased need for-91
Grief
  How long it will last-
    17, 25, 75
  Passages-6, 77, 111
  Process-19, 23, 35, 53,
    103, 113, 121
  Recovery-
    25, 39, 57, 59, 85, 89
  Response-31, 45
Growth-73, 119
Guilt-23, 89

Healing-21, 29, 65, 75, 79, 89, 91, 93, 105, 121
Human, being-31

Identifying feelings-27
Illness-49, 125
Insomnia-37, 125
Intruding thoughts-23
Irrational beliefs-19

Loneliness-93, 107
Longing for lost love-117
Loss-4, 5, 21, 23, 29, 33, 35, 37, 49, 53, 55, 61, 73, 75, 85, 87, 101, 105, 109, 115, 117
Losses, secondary-63
Love-111, 115, 117

Medication-37
Memories-87, 95, 115
Motivation-23

Normal-59
Normal grief response
    Cognitive-19, 23
    Emotional-17, 103

Obsessions-23, 61

Pain-19, 21, 25, 35, 39, 51, 53, 91, 119, 123
Patience-31, 113
Permission to grieve-17
Personality-45
Possessions-87
Primary care physician-37, 125, 126
Psychiatrist-37
Purpose-117

Questioning-23, 61, 101, 109, 125

Reaching out-65, 123
Recurring reminders of loss-51, 77, 87, 103
Remembering-51, 83, 95, 115
Rest, need for-49
Roles, changed-63

Self-esteem-23
Self-talk-23, 33, 89, 107
Sexuality-45, 85, 125
Shock-17
Simple truths-79, 105, 111
Sleep disturbances-35, 37, 125
Social impact of death-107
Spirituality-37, 67, 73, 91, 125
Stress-61, 85
Support systems-39, 65, 67
Surviving-21, 31, 33, 53, 79
Symbols-75

Tasks-19, 101
Thoughts of loved one-
23, 51, 83, 95, 103, 113, 115
Time-
17, 19, 25, 47, 63, 73,
87, 91, 93, 107
Trusting-109

Unfinished business-83

Wounds, emotional-17, 29

 Bereavement Express

A heartfelt way to express your condolences to a relative, friend, co-worker, or client

---

Sending cards and flowers may express your sympathy. Sending *A Different Season* lets others know that you want to help.

= ☒   Your order is received.

📖   A copy of A Different Season: A Practical Guide for Growth While Grieving a Death, by Joseph Robert Pfeiffer, LCSW, G.T. is selected.

✍   A message from you is personally handwritten on a card.

✎   The book is autographed by the author (if desired).

❀   The book is gift-wrapped.

☒   The book is sent via USPS Priority Mail to the bereaved within 24 hours, and can also be mailed book rate.

Bereavement Express
Order Form
Fax (901) 726-4495

Please send a copy of *A Different Season*

This is an expression of my/our condolence. Please include the following message:

_____

_____

_____

Signed – (PLEASE PRINT) _____

Author to personally sign book? ❏ Yes ❏ No

Mail To: (PLEASE PRINT)

Name _____

Address _____

City _____ State _____ Zip _____

COST

❏ $16.95 (Shipped USPS Priority Mail within 24 hours)

❏ $13.95 (Shipped USPS via book rate within 48 hours)

❏ .90 Include sales tax for each book ONLY if you are living in TN

TOTAL _____

Your Name _____

Address _____

City _____ State _____ Zip _____

Telephone (   ) _____ E-Mail _____

Mail to: Landscapes Publishing • P.O. Box 820650 • Memphis, TN 38182-0650
(901) 578-9107 • Fax: (901) 726-4495 • E-Mail:Sales@LandscapesPublishing.com